CIVILIZING ME

Sany Varghese

For my grandmother and father
who are no more with us;
They left a hole in our hearts
that we packed
with stories and memories.

Forget the former things;
do not dwell on the past.

See, I am doing a new thing!
Now it springs up;
Do you not perceive it?

I am making a way in the desert
and streams in the wasteland.

Table of Contents

FLOWERS AND BUTTERFLIES

Nature's Way

A leaf swaying in the wind
has no care or wear.
It darkens and veins
with the wind and rain.

A bud that blossoms
knows not its end.
It yields its scent
and cares not its loss.

A wave splashing on the sand
is soon restrained.
It repeats its attempts
even when the tide is low.

Spring rushes in.
Summer holds it back.
Autumn prepares the coming
of Winter.

What can man do
with Nature's sway?
Yield and Renew.
It's Nature's way.

The Morning Sun

A child wakes early with the rising sun.
Both gleeful and ready to have some fun.

With squeals and shrills she bumbles down.
Skips over dolls and lolling heads.

She chases goats and yanks their tails.
Then grabs the chicks searching for worms.

The morning sun chuckles and winks.
Shines a bright ray on this irreverent child.

The clever butterflies give good chase
but stop on a branch and the child gets a wing.

The drooping plants stir and sway
as they charm and eye the morning sun.

The naughty child pulls their outstretched arms
steals their fruit and blooming flower.

The gentle cows moo and amble along.
She squeezes their udders and laughs at the squirt.

The grass is green and fresh for the picking
so the gracious cows just keep on grazing.

The morning sun, youthful and debonair
flirts with the clouds and tranquil air.

Tree and leaf at her mercy.
She taunts and laughs as they beg for light.

Her favorite sport.
Watch the merry child
pluck the flowers and eat the fruit
chase the chickens and tease the birds.

When the day is done and it's time for bed

the evening sun comes with a heavy haze
and beckons her young sun over the canopied sky.

The child runs home for bed and bath
and tales of fun with the morning sun.

Mama on her stoop sips her tea,
lets the day's toil flow from her
like a gentle wave.

The evening sun retreats with a kiss on her brow.
She closes her eyes and sleep steals the night.

Up the Garden Path

Where the lilies grow
the daisies nod
the Susans laze.

Where the streams flow
the stones knock
the snows melt.

Where the valley hides
the soft meadow
the scented flowers.

To the abandoned grotto
of buried treasures.
Forbidden. Wild. Silent.

Parents, look away

Watch the feet of little children.

They often stray

when parents look away.

They splash into puddles

with laughs and giggles.

They chase butterflies across fields

as if their feet could tuck

and their arms turn to wings.

Watch the little feet at play
to learn the science of many things.
They scamper over rocks and stones
climb trees and hills
like goats and rams
when parents look away.

They pick the berry purple and ripe
and press them into their mouths.
With teeth stained they continue their game.
There's so much more fun and play
when parents look away.

Have you seen the little feet
when they see a lake?
They rush to it with squeals.
Tiny fingers try to catch the fish.
The ones that wiggle and tease
and make the children screech.

Oh parents can you look away
so little feet can go
where they want
and not be stuffed
into boots and shoes
laced and tied
like yours and mine?

In the Shed, In the Bed

The hen gathers her chicks under her wings.
The farmer herds his sheep into the pen.
The horses trot their way to the stable.
The cows walk their way to the byre.

With a heavy groan I grieve the loss of a day.
In quiet reflection I wonder about the next.
With tender resignation I accept them both.

The hen closes her eyes and the chicks relax.
The farmer turns off the light. The sheep rest.
The horses soften their legs ready for sleep.
The cows ease their stare and chew the cud.

Silence covers us all like a sheet.

The Cedar and Oak

Tall Magnificent
Scraping the skies and clouds.
Air lighter
sounds softer
swinging and swaying
with the breeze and the wind.

Gnarly Wide
Mired in soil and dirt
Air thicker
noises louder
grinding and groaning
with the weight and the struggle.

The shoot and the root
both part of the mighty
Cedar and Oak.

NOSTALGIC

The Almari

Grandma kept her precious things
hidden in the Almari.

Shiny with a polished look
Silken and smooth
flush against the wall.
A secret store of treasured things.

No deft hand or envious glance
could find a way into its contents.

Stock-still and bolted.
Unyielding as a fortress.
Protecting my Grandma's wealth
and things she cherished.

Never left open
except for a purpose.
No stray eye could wander
or catch a quick peek.

I imagined their contents -
Jewels, gems
pots of gold.
Letters, notes
from lovers of old.

I admired its tranquil state.
Locked up
like a Count in exile
full of pride and worth.

With its paneled chest
rippling with wealth and power
it taunted and goaded me.

I'd learnt to take a casual glimpse
whenever I walked into the room
to see if the key hung on the lock

and I could be so bold.

When Granny sent me with key
to swing that formidable chest open
I went with eager excitement
to see the treasures within.

Shelves of unequal sizes.
Whiffs of fragrant smells
some bold, others very faint.
Stacks of paper and clothes.
neatly placed and tagged.

My task was small
but responsibility heavy.
Find her special luxury soap
round and large
tucked deep inside
and far behind.

The Almaris in the bedroom
had an established hierarchy
that matched their presumed wealth.

The steel Almaris often lay open
with a key and chain
hanging low from their bellies.
They were loud and made bitter sounds

cranky and clanging like mean old women.

Like a harem they waited
in the bedroom
to be chosen
but everybody knew who was held
with the highest regard.

The wooden Almari
Elegant and smooth to the touch
fragrant as a garden of lilies
full of mystery and aura
the Magnificent one.
Silent with the superior air
of the Matriarch.

After Grandma passed away
and I a child no more
I had no interest in the Almari anymore.

My childhood fantasies
and flirtations of youth
were a memory of the past.
Strange and faded.

Seeing my valley green

A river runs through the valley.
The gentle hills on either flank
are lush meadows sprinkled with wildflowers.
The goats and sheep graze happily.

The houses come alive at night
like tiny stars in the blackened sky.
Smoke stacks puff out their fumes.
Like Dad with his cigar and bellowing voice.

When the dewy day breaks
women with linen bands on their heads
spill out of homes with buckets.
Like Mom on a Saturday morning.

In the pale afternoon light
children come out to play
kicking a ball or just squealing about.
Like my little brother in his flouncy shorts.

Once verdant and full of youthful vigor
now empty and desolate.
Overwhelmed by loss and people no more
My valley lies low in shadows deep.

Cabin on the mountains

On the misty mountain
smoothly over rock
flow the gentle falls.
Heaving up the cliff
roots catch the fall.

In the wooden cabin
knotty eyes keep watch.
Forest scents like vapor
float from room to room.

In the upstairs loft
secret treasures wait.

Trees embrace the pasture.
Meadow gives space
to stretch and ease.
Still waters mirror
the peace of the soul.

The gravel path slows the motor
to a crawl.
No fire, no storm, no cry, no wail
could speed the flow
over this stony trail.

Let it roll forward or backward
or not at all.

The air is cool.
The mountains quiet.

We rev the engine
and head back to the fold.

In the Desert

Hot and dry.

    The clay oven with burning coals

    where Mama would cook Kuboos

    and serve with lamb and mutton.

Swirling wind gusts.

    The breezy beach

    where we'd go to cool off in the summer

    and my sister would hunt for treasures

    hidden in the fishing boats.

Golden dunes of sand.

    Roller coasters undulating

like waves into the distant sky.
Tossed up shoes and clothes
leaving a trail of dust and thrill.

Slim busty date trees.
Mangroves full
of sensuous flavors and pleasures.
Baskets of figs and pistachio nuts.
Such jolly picnics with family and friends.

Bubbling springs of water.
Glorious fountains
that leap and flash their brilliant light.
Slaking our thirst
refreshing our scorched bodies.

In the desert stands a little shrub
thriving on the ancient sands.

Time captured

Time is like a vapor.

In a coffee cup or a photograph
A souvenir or a blanket
A warm embrace, a cold stare
A fire on the stove
A smell of smoke in the air
In travel maps and journals.

In the prison
In a garden
On a sofa or the kitchen
In our childhood
In our children's eyes
Wherever you've been
Whatever you've wanted
Time captures.

It comes
as a guest uninvited.
It goes
as one who stayed.

CONFLICTED

The Couple

My dog and I
leisurely walk in the neighborhood.
The flowing breeze curls our tresses
and tugs at our cheeks.
With a bright wide smile I say -
Hello neighbors!
What a lovely day to be out for a walk.

They fuss and tease.
He jumps and licks
and enjoys the day's thrills
with bark and chase.

The evening walk is the social milieu
of nods and smiles.
Arms and legs swinging
with vigor and health
and bounteous energy.

At a distance, I spy the couple
as they take their walk
in the neighborhood.
Man in ecru woman in burgundy.
I know them by the colors.

Man's head slightly askew in expectation
of the usual nods and smiles.
Woman a step behind.
Left arm swinging, anxious.
Keeping the half step between them.

The Man and his wife
foreigners in this land
out of step with the mores
of the town and hood.
Skittish and eager for
acknowledgment and worth.

Two chattering girls walk by
ignoring his tentative wave.
The wife flashes a quick smile,
whispers a joke to the Man.
He attempts a mirthless laugh.

I watch, my dog and I
as they turn and walk up their driveway.
Man's arm swinging wildly, annoyed.
Wife rushing in, draws the blinds.

Fear of the Night

Picking up the lantern
the boy treads fearfully
towards the barn.

He hears his footsteps.
They sound slow and stealthy
like a thief at night.

Surprised by the visit
the creatures in the barn
scurry away in a hurry.
Others rush forward to receive the light.

He heads to the loft
frightened by everything.
Searches, and finds it
where he knew it always was.

Putting out the lantern
the boy heads home
into the soundless night.

How peaceful it is
when all is quiet and still
in the dead of night.

Relief

I watch the bricks
open wide and crumble -
my life's worth
of forming and making.

I watch the bricks
shatter and tumble -
my life's worth
of laying and cementing.

I watch the bricks
crash with a rumble -
my life's worth
of hoping and dreaming.

Such irrepressible relief
to see my worthless striving
fall and crumble
without a grumble.

The Guard

I keep my senses alert.

I listen, lean in, pay heed

to all that's said, intended and suggested.

The innuendoes and insults,

the whispered threats and angry glances,

the surreptitious moves and hoodwinks,

the suppressed emotions of hate and ill will.

I ignore the sweet honeyed words,
exchanged between lovers or friends,
family or colleagues.
Friendly gestures and words
are of no interest to me.
People smiling and carefree,
holding hands or bursting with laughter,
they are of little consequence.
They are empty and don't carry the weight or value
of my time or interest.

I'm wary and suspicious
of the danger and evil
that surrounds me.
The prowlers who wait
to catch the unsuspecting and vulnerable.
My sword is drawn, my bow is bent
ready for action.

The laughing crowd sees me
and comments on my wary manner.
My suspicious glance and cautious steps.
It makes me angry to see their suspicion.
My anger turns to rage.
I charge and send a vicious blow
toward an unsuspecting victim.
Unraveled, I search the crowd for others.

The Long view

If we could view Earth from the moon
It would be so fascinating.
    Vast lands, great rivers
    sharp peaks, deep valleys

If we could observe people from afar
It would be quite enthralling.
    Jubilant, exultant
    Lonely, abandoned

If we could view cells through a microscope
It would be so wondrous.
    Invisible, silent
    Mysterious, remote

If we could fly over the Serengeti
It would be so thrilling.
    The wonderful and mighty
    moving in harmony
    with creatures
    graceful, small, and swift

If
If

Our hearts yearn and long
hope and want
    for fascination and enthrallment.

Our hearts ache and hurt
    with loneliness and abandonment.

Maybe we ought to take the long view
over our Serengeti
then what's here may look
Like *the one* out there.

Maybe.

IN STRIDE

Civilizing me

I have no desire for these things
you speak of so highly
that force me out
of the comfort of my life
my surroundings and people
into a train of great expectations.

I hear it rumbling past each morning
as I watch the sun rise
and feel relief that I'm not in there.

Rushing to some place
to do something
that I don't wish to do.

I am not in distress.
I don't need deliverance.
I'm not in the pursuit of your dreams for me.
So please let me be
where I am happy
and want to be.

I can sow and reap
on my own land
and find pleasure
in the slow yield of my crop.
Right here is where I want to be.

In Pairs they march

Wisdom and Prudence -
stuck up twins I thought.
Always preening and prettying themselves
in their haute couture dresses.

Indignation and Judgment -
with their fiery breaths
go riding their chariots
ready for war and terror.

Promises and Vows -
The subservient lot
cower barefoot in ashes and sashes
speaking of gloom and doom
Oh these pairs of silly twins.

It's wild country here -
Wild and Untainted
by Civility or Kindness.

They ride roughshod over land and sea
Plundering and Pillaging
Killing and Murdering
the Poor and Wretched
Weak and Vulnerable.

Like Hedonists and Voyeurs,
they hop about like two fat bunnies.
Such terrible pairs they are.

The Vessel of good comportment

It stands brazen and tall
buffed and polished.
In shining armor
ready for the Lady's use.

Mouth rimmed as a flute.
Mute - no words pour forth
until in the Lady's hand
it comes alive with spirit and vigor.

Tinkling and teasing

the Lady wraps her fingers around
and coils it like a snake.
Graceful and sinewy in poise and gait.

Wine and laughter
mixed with venom and brandy.
The chalice is filled
ready for the Lady's use.

The clock strikes twelve.
The bells start to toll.
The vessel empties its contents
into its unsuspecting target.

Now back in the Lady's hand
the vessel with its good comportment
stands tall and assuredly.
An envy of all the ladies.

The New Ambassador

In crisp uniform and leather pouch
the ambassador walked up the runway
towards the waiting crowd
hands extended in eager anticipation.

A pivotal moment of change
spiking, desperate.
A new generation seeking
a new alliance
a break from the old.

A moment of conflict
flashes on her face
then gradually eases.

Tall and willowy she holds
her poise and grace.

A vain endeavor
was how they viewed it.
She let that slide.
Her strength of purpose
came from within.
Steely and tested.

A voice in the audience shot off a cry
of exultation.
Others followed with a thunderous roar.
The mutiny had begun.

No words crossed the lips
of the ambassador.
The voices of the swelling multitude
spoke volumes.

Freedom

Escorted out through the high metal fence
he staggers
clutching a small bag of belongings.
His, from years past.

The first light hits like a lightning bolt
and jerks him from his stupor.
Fear rises like acid from his bowels
and stings his eyes.

He starts to hobble piteously
towards the dirt road
dragging his yoke of shame.

Suddenly he stops.
Looks back for a brief glance.
Tosses his bag and starts to run
into the dazzling morning light.

AFFLICTED

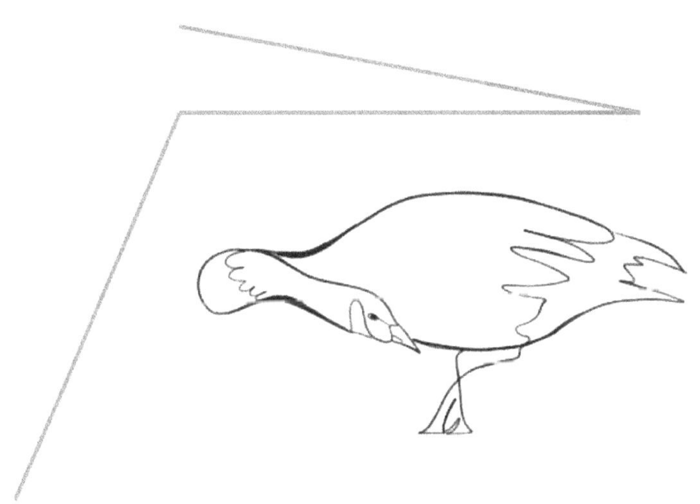

Demon of the night

It yanks and tugs
at the poor woman's joints
twisted with ache
throb and sigh.

It grinds the mortar
with a callous pestle
as she moans and groans
with waves of pain.

Held at bay in her youth.
Now no strength left
to fight.
She yields and watches it
wield a merciless attack.

Snatching sleep and blankets
off to the floor.
Throwing pillows and warm pads
out to the side.

In the still of the night
The Demon plays a ruthless game.
Then cackles and crows
amused at her plight.

Tethered all day
by the unassailable Dawn
the night is its time
to wreak havoc and pain.

It chases the runt
the sick and weak.
Savage and insatiable
for thrill and glee.

Like a coward it works
in the shadows

for fear of encounter
or any reprisal.

Like shifting sands
her weary mind slips and slides
seeking escape from the iron chains.
Heavy and clanging
with twinges and pangs.

The clock has no urge
to hurry along
so she stares it down
till it yields and loudly chimes
the passage of time.

Faster, faster she says -
I can't last much longer.
The quiet the silence
The darkness and gloom.
Hurry!

When Dawn comes
the demons of the night slip away.
Like taunting devils out for fun
They get their share
and leave her there.

The Main artery

The boy was skipping to town
jiggling change in his pocket
when the gunfire started.

He quickly dashed for cover
as his mother had instructed him.

An hour later he rose fearfully from his cover
ears and eyes shell shocked
and rushed back home.

Over a body lay his weeping mother.
His father's.
The main artery of his family.
Through which had flowed
their very breath.

The boy walks over
wraps his arms around his mother
and starts to pour love and comfort
into her sorrowful heart.
Sealing the broken artery.

Woe to the Silent

No light can streak through.
No joy can cross.
No blue skies no starry nights.
Even the planets lie hidden
Silent behind the canopy of your dark cloud.

Woe to you my child.
The vastness of the universe
The majesty of nature
The twinkling of the morning star
The call of the hummingbird
All stay silent behind your curtain of despair.

Rise!
Listen to their stories of courage and splendor
Grace and valor
Let them rent the curtain
that fell that summer's day
And silenced your joy and wonder.

A Lover's Grief

Turns to wretchedness,
anger mixed with grief.
All that love and nurture
yielded only wild rebellion.

Rage uncontrolled breaks the dam
of patience and restraint.
Judgment and justice strike
with an iron hand.

No more room left for
compassion or mercy,
forgiveness or love,

generosity or kindness.
The hand of wrath swings hard.

The loved is left
devastated and wretched,
subdued and subjugated.
Cowering in a corner.

The lover's fence of protection
shattered and leveled.

Exposed to the predators.
Eyes cast down moaning in
fear and trepidation.

The lover's raging heart
relieved and sated.
The loved heart
trodden and worn.

The lover pours out his liquid love.
to salve the wounded heart
singing songs of
love and yearning,
groaning in
misery and remorse.

Discontent

Beautiful gowns of
claret and gold
turquoise and silver.
Bonnets and hats
blazing and brilliant
with ribbons and colors.

Locks of hair
falling like tresses.
Lips so lush -
full and inviting.
A kiss from a Prince
or even a Count will do.

My Cinderella life -
hapless and hopeless
heavily draped in
cinder and ash.
Darkly I dream.

Glitter and gaiety,
laughter and thrill,
tinkles and tinsels.
Mansions and fences
valets and butlers.

Walls of tapestries,
rugs of Persian silk,
caviar and aged wine.
A life of luxury.

Dressed in fine silk.
Feet in glass slippers,
gushing with joy
I step out in gold.

Graceful and light
like a swan
gliding in a lake.

Tick tock.
Tick tock.

The clock strikes twelve.

Back by the chimney
in soot and rags.
No joy no shine
ne'er more will I see.

Tick tock.
Tick tock.

Misery has me
wrapped in a tight swaddle.
Despair
watches in stony silence.
My lonely heart
wretches in guilt and sorrow.

Tick tock.
Tick tock.

Dreams and fantasies.

Discontent.

The Long tail

Peeking through the curtain of my hiding spot
I noticed a long streak of dirt
leading to the garden
which I know leads to the fountain
where coins are dropped for luck.
Luck that comes only for the lucky.

I leave that spot and follow the path
to the house next door.
A mansion of turrets and spires.
My sister's schoolmate lives there

with all the trappings of a rich life.
I move on as the gardener has seen me.

I take Main Street to the little alley
where I usually kick the ball with my friends
on warm Sunday evenings.
It's quiet and empty.
I wait for some company.
It's a Friday and they are in the mosque.

Hunger starts to growl in my belly
so I follow the path to the street vendor
that sells falafels.
He gives me a hot one and a soda.
I'm happy and keep walking.

I like the quiet, but also long for a friend
to walk around with.
I see a mangy dog digging for scraps.
He looks more desperate than me.
I have seen him often so I call him my friend.

My parents will be home now.
They will be talking in whispers
as if each word is too precious to let drop.
I feel their groans and sighs.
They smile though we have nothing to smile about.

We sought refuge in this country
for freedom and opportunity
but poverty and destitution followed.
My life will reflect the long tail of suffering
that follows the sad choices my parents had to make.
I walk on to meet its end.

RIVERS AND BASINS

Look Beyond

Look up when you're down -
or your sorrow will drag you
into deep despair.

Look down when you're up -
or your haughty eyes will miss
the sudden plunge of the meteor.

Or look far beyond -
to behold the majestic wave.
The rise and dip of the glorious sun.

With its cheery arc crowning our morning
and the gentle amber gaze blessing our evening.
No fanfare no audience
No pomp or splendor.

Just a peek -
of the crimson yonder.

Hold a Reserve

Famine comes to us all.
Some fear it all their life
so freeze and lie
like possums dead.

Famine comes to us all.
Some unaware
bound and frolic
like doe and buck
without a care.

Famine is on its way.
Some store the grain
and hold a reserve.
To use and enjoy
as they want.

A Swinging time

A kite
with no string
floats with the wind.

The old banyan tree hides
its merry swing,
the floating cloud
its lightness of being.

No will to please
It dances gaily
swinging on the hips
of the laughing wind.

A Nod of Remembrance

A Day of Remembrance
of hopes and dreams
born from innocence
now dead or dying
from life's travails.

A Day of Remembrance
of people and places
cherished and pure

full in life
not absent in death.

A Day of Remembrance
of tales and memories
imagined and real
fading and light
like parchments old.

But today!
Its a nod
and off I go
to the day at hand.

Wise

A drowning heart
knows
but cares not.

An aching heart
cares
but knows not.

A wise heart
knows and cares.

It neither
aches nor drowns.
For neither are wise
to consider.

River of Life

Torrents of rain pour in
beating down
swelling up.

The basin fills with tears and sorrow
and spills on the riverbanks.

Thirsty plants breathe with new life
quenched of their dying thirst.

Peace comes to the river and plants.
for a while
for a season
before the cycle repeats.

Acknowledgements

My husband said I should do it.
I said No.
He insisted
so I did it.

He is right half the time.
I usually prefer the other half.

My sincere gratitude to Lindsey Chastain for her valuable
feedback and edits, and to Esther Rai for her wonderful
illustrations.

9 7 9 8 8 1 5 2 1 8 5 6 7